T0129419

YOU
ARE THE
CREATOR

Seven Powerful
Principles
to
Engineer
the
Life You Deserve

Derrick Fennell

BALBOA.
PRESS

A DIVISION OF HAY HOUSE

Balboa Press books may be ordered through booksellers or by contacting:

Balboa Press
A Division of Hay House
1663 Liberty Drive
Bloomington, IN 47403
www.balboapress.com
1 (877) 407-4847

Print information available on the last page.

ISBN: 978-1-5043-9640-0 (sc)
ISBN: 978-1-5043-9642-4 (hc)
ISBN: 978-1-5043-9641-7 (e)

Library of Congress Control Number: 2018901206

Balboa Press rev. date: 02/06/2018

Contents

Acknowledgment

As I researched the subject matter and content of this book, many individuals were instrumental in helping me. Many thanks go out to all who assisted in that process with your ideas, comments, thoughts, and support.

Acknowledgments

Introduction

How many times have we had great thoughts or ideas that we never acted on? How many times have we reflected on those ideas and said to ourselves "I should have" or "I wish I had"? How many times have we observed those ideas in action years later by someone else who had the courage and the confidence to act? This book analyzes the dynamics surrounding the seven power principles of how you can engineer the life you deserve, and it is designed to inspire you to act today.

Dare To Be Who You Are!

Dictionary.com defines the word *success* in this way: "the favorable or prosperous termination of attempts or endeavors; the accomplishment of one's goals."

Success is a subjective, relative term in that it means different things for different people. For some, the word *success* could mean ascertaining a certain financial status, to others it could mean finding the love of their lives, and to some it could mean just living a certain lifestyle or accomplishing a long-awaited event. For example, this could be reaching a ninetieth birthday or making the Olympic team; success for some could be earning a six-figure income. For others, such as former President Barack Obama, success factors included becoming the President of the United States of America. Success as an indicator changes as we accomplish our goals in life. Whatever *your* definition of success is for your personal life, you must first define what your desires in life are and then take the necessary steps to achieve the goals that will lead you to engineering the life you deserve.

Dreams Do Come True!

Can you remember when you were a young child wanting to learn how to ride a bike? Can you remember the fear of possibly falling off the bike and getting hurt? Even our parents were afraid for us and therefore would typically put training wheels on our bikes to help us balance. But when those training wheels came off our bikes and we had to attempt riding them without those training wheels, our hearts would pump with excitement, as well as the fear of falling and getting hurt. However, we would not let that deter us from trying. Our desire, passion, faith, and belief were so strong, driving us to overcome the fear factor and take the action of attempting to ride our bikes until we were successful. Despite the many times we fell, we would reevaluate, adjust, and get back up on that bike and try it again. Those same principles that we utilized in our formidable years are the same principles required to live the lives we desire.

Many people have a fear of success, as well as a fear of the responsibilities and the expectations that will come with success. An example is a need to change and leave behind associates who are not conducive to or who do not embrace the lives we so passionately desire and crave for ourselves, our families, and those around us. Many times this leads us to making new friends and associates who accept, encourage, and fully support our dreams, desires, and accomplishments. There is a law of entropy (the tendency of things to decline or deteriorate over time). A basic law of physics is that nothing is static. Things are either growing or declining, and how that translates into relationships is that some we will outgrow or some will tend to cause us to remain static and decline into toxic relationships. That fear or reluctance comes in many different forms. Some people aren't even aware they have these fears. They sometimes just cannot bring themselves to act, or they unknowingly perform self-sabotaging acts that keep them in the places or situations they are working so hard to leave.

Some people have a fear of failure. They are afraid to step outside of their comfort zones and face their insecurities. For example, we all know someone who must control every decision, large and small, at home or in his or her business. Sometimes the business cannot grow or the home cannot become the wonderful, restful place it was meant to be because someone has the need to control and cannot move out of the usual comfort zone. The result is a failed or obsolete business or a failed or unhappy home.

However, failing is not finite. Failing should be viewed as an opportunity to learn something about yourself and provide an opportunity to improve upon who you are. An example of this is Lebron James and the 2010 Miami Heat basketball team. Lebron James left his home state of Ohio and the Cleveland Cavilers NBA franchise in search of an NBA championship. The team he left had the best winning record of the NBA for the two previous consecutive years but could never move past the playoffs. The Miami Heat were successful in recruiting Lebron James, the most valuable player (MVP) of the NBA, and all-star center Chris Bosh to join another all-star player and Dwayne Wade, former world champion of the Miami Heat. These men were also champions together on the 2008 USA Olympic basketball team. The 2010 Miami Heat had put together a team that was so formidable that they predicted themselves to win the 2010 NBA championship even before one game had been played.

As history has recorded, they made it to the championship series, but they were swept. Lebron James, Chris Bosh, Dwayne Wade, and the Miami Heat were not supposed to lose the championship; that would be considered a failure. This loss caused such an embarrassment to the Heat franchise and the players because of their arrogance and disrespect toward the other professional NBA teams. As a result, this loss caused Lebron James and his teammates to reevaluate their approach to that season, their personal commitment to success, and their character flaws. The failure of the team to live up to its potential and their own expectations presented an excellent opportunity for them to reevaluate their mistakes and step out of their comfort zones to reinvent themselves. As a result, they went on to win two consecutive NBA championship titles.

World-renowned inventor Thomas Edison stated, "I have not failed. I have merely found ten thousand ways that won't work." The truth of the matter is that you never truly fail at anything until you decide to give up and quit. This is the only time a failure is finite.

In the early days of Kentucky Fried Chicken, the founder, Colonel Sanders, was selling his recipe for cooking chicken to other chicken restaurateurs. Those who cook often think their own recipes are the best. Now imagine going to those restaurateurs who are selling their own style of food and trying to convince them that your recipe is better for them. Colonel Sanders was turned down over one thousand times before he got his first sale. After each rejection, he would reevaluate his presentation and modify it to incorporate potential rejections and responses. Imagine the commitment required for his success. Imagine the feeling of being rejected one thousand times. I ask you this question: "Would you have given up on your idea after being rejected one thousand times?" He didn't, and as a result, he didn't fail, for he never quit. In this concept is a valuable nugget, one that I often found myself sharing with my grandchildren as I helped mold and shape their thoughts about their lives. I would tell them that a winner never quits and a quitter never wins.

We have all heard that the definition of ignorance is doing the same things repeatedly and expecting different results. But Sanders was not an ignorant man. He applied common sense. He would always review his results, evaluate the errors, make the adjustments, and modify his presentation as necessary. This is one of many examples of commitment to your dreams, whatever they may be. Take this moment and think of someone you know who was that committed to a cause, a purpose, and would not be denied.

I often think of individuals who had to overcome impossible odds to achieve the dream. For instance, Martin Luther King's dream inspired a people and a nation to reevaluate themselves and end the segregated ways of America. Nelson Mandela's cause and dream was so powerful that he endured twenty-seven years in prison under the rule of apartheid, only to survive and become the president of South Africa and lead the revolution to end apartheid. So I submit to you that there is power in your dreams, the power to change the world for the betterment of all.

However, your dream life doesn't have to be a change-the-world kind of undertaking. It can start small. It starts with you and your personal desires, passions, faith, and belief. It starts with your maybe just wanting to run and complete a marathon or taking your kids on a special trip to some place you or they have never been. Or maybe it means celebrating a special event with your spouse or preparing yourself for that career you always wanted and getting it. Whatever those dreams are, the seeds are in you to do it. Otherwise, the thought would have never come to the forefront of your mind.

I once read a quote by Zig Ziglar that went something like this: "You don't have to be great to start, but you have to start in order to be great." I'm reminded of another well-known quote: "When the student is ready to learn, the teacher will appear." So embrace the thoughts, the learning process, and the learning curves you may endure, but don't give up on your dreams or the champion in you.

There is a champion in each of us. The battle is not external but internal, and you have the power to win and live that dream life. It's only a matter of your level of commitment to your desire, passion, faith, and belief. The proof of this is all around you. How many people have you heard of who came from nowhere, only to achieve an incredible dream life? Most have heard Oprah Winfrey's story and Tyler Perry's story. These are stories of overcoming insurmountable odds and going on to live a dream life, a life that has impact and makes a difference. There are many such stories all around you, in your schools, in your neighborhoods, in your churches, and even in your families.

I think of my grandparents who grew up on a small farm in North Carolina in the early 1900s. My grandmother's father worked in a coal mine and was killed in a mining accident, leaving behind a wife, and six small children. Now, if you can, imagine the odds of an African American widowed mother raising six small kids alone in the early 1900s. But her desire, passion, faith, and belief for her children's success was so strong that she would not consider failure as an option. There were many struggles and hard times, but she overcame them, and all her children finished school, with four of the six going on to graduate from college. That was her dream.

We have all heard of individuals running a marathon and hitting that imaginary brick wall, the point where your body shuts down and you can't seem to take another step. Then there are those individuals who reach down deep inside and find an inner strength that allows them to break through that brick wall and keep going when the odds are against them. In the 1950s, it was believed that it was impossible for a man to run a mile in under four minutes. Then it happened, and today it's common for individuals to run a mile in under four minutes.

There are so many examples around us. Everywhere we look we can see individuals overcoming insurmountable odds. I think of Arsenio Hall, who was the first African American to host a late-night television show. Here's a man who had the belief in his dream and went after it. He stated that he was inspired from watching The Tonight Show, hosted by Johnny Carson.

What about Michael Jordan, who was cut from his tenth-grade basketball team only to go on and follow his dream, becoming recognized as the greatest player to play the game of basketball on a professional level. The point that I'm making is that on the other side of all our fears lies all our dreams, waiting to come true. So never give up on your dreams, regardless of your obstacles.

The power of visualization is a very powerful concept. This concept allows you to see yourself where you want to be. To quote Dr. Martin Luther King, "If the mind can conceive it, you can achieve it." This concept is about the power of visualizing exactly what you want, how you want it, where you want it, and why you want it. See yourself and visualize yourself in that place you want to be.

Here are a few important action steps you can do right now. Write down your visualization. Review it every day first thing in the morning and the last thing at night. Put together a poster collage; gather movies, stories that are inspiring and that represent the desired state so that the pictures can become concrete and real in your mind. Also visit people, places, or things that represent your goals—for example, that neighborhood that has million-dollar homes, or Yankee Stadium, or Carnegie Hall, or a Broadway show, or Wall Street. Take the opportunity to be in the presence of the person who has the biggest influence and imitate the things that represents the accomplishment of your dreams. These steps are so important to engineering your vision. You will begin to see yourself as a person entitled to these dreams because you have and are doing the work required of you. Nothing can withstand consistent effort applied over time. Never give up. Just believe you will succeed.

I can remember growing up in my grandparent's home as a young adolescent. They were entrepreneurs, and I wanted to own my own company. I didn't really know what kind of company, but I wanted to run my own business. When I was buying my first home at age twenty-one, I discovered the business in which I wanted to get involved. I wanted to own a real estate company. I began to learn about that industry and aligned myself with individuals who were in the industry. Soon I was a real estate agent and on my way to carving out my own business in the mortgage industry.

The main point here is that if you see yourself doing whatever you desire in life and meditate on it with conviction and believe you can achieve it, I'm here to tell you that you can. This is a very important step. It allows you to transfer your visual thoughts to a concrete and tangible form. Truly this is a very powerful concept, and many people underestimate the value of this nugget. This element alone could possibly be the determining factor that stops you from being the creator and engineer of the life you deserve. There is a saying amongst highly successful people who are at the top of their fields: "Successful people do what unsuccessful people are unwilling to do." So write those visual thoughts down and read them first thing every day and last thing every night. This allows the conviction and meditation process to manifest itself into your life. Successful business owners do this all the time. They use the business plan as a road map to success. This begins that process of developing your road map to the life you deserve.

Once you have the picture in your mind, carefully nurture and guard that dream, that vision. Nurturing the dream means thinking, visualizing, and meditating on the dream; seeing +the outcomes of the dream; reading what you can on topics that can help you work toward your desires; and never allowing others to steal your dreams. This means carefully guarding your psyche against those who will criticize or cast doubt upon your desires. There is a difference between those who offer constructive criticism or advice with your best interests in mind—those whose intentions are to point out potential risks so that you can create alternatives or avoid them entirely—and those who nurture underlying feelings of jealousy or who are threatened by the changes that come from your achieving your goals. In this same light are those people who, through their use of negative language or emotional turmoil, create a negative association with your dreams, thus stealthily crushing all good feelings associated with your desires.

Maya Angelou was interviewed on *The Oprah Winfrey Show* and talked about a person who was invited to her house party. This person was using foul/negative language in her home, and she asked him to leave. She said that words are physical things and that his words were physical things spewing out of his mouth and falling on her floor, contaminating the good energy of her home. We must all guard against those who spew garbage, contaminating our minds and dreams with negative energy.

This point reminds me of a slogan by the United Negro Collegiate Fund (UNCF). Each year during their fund-raising program, the main theme is that a mind is a terrible thing to waste. This is so true, and it goes right to the heart and purpose of this book.

The goal of this book is to encourage, enlighten, and empower you to realize the creativity of your mind and how your dominant thoughts have impact on your current circumstances, regardless of where you are today. All decisions begin with a thought. All actions and inactions are the results of those thoughts. What's important to understand about this knowledge is the fact that you are in total control of the results of your thoughts. With that understanding lies the true power of who you are and what your capabilities can become. *You are the creator.*

Avoid negative people, for they are the greatest destroyers of self-confidence and self-esteem.

Surround yourself with people who bring out the best in you.

This book first requires you to interpret and comprehend the seven powerful principles of creating the life you deserve. Without first understanding these principles and the reason they are important for you to succeed is like taking a road trip and not mapping out the directions to get to your destination. You will start your trip and you may get there, but it's a high probability that you won't—and certainly not in a timely fashion. These principles must be adhered to in the order listed. The seven principles are as follows:

1. Desire

2. Passion

3. Faith

4. Belief

5. Action

6. Reevaluation

7. Adjustment

Let's evaluate the characteristics of the seven powerful principles and identify the actions required of you to engineer the life you deserve.

Be Realistic Wish the Impossible

Paulo Coelho,
The Alchemist

Notes

Chapter 1

Principle of Desire

Desire is the first of the seven principles you must have. Without desire, when those tough times come—and they will come—you will want to give up and quit. It is the principle of desire that drives you through those tough times, the desire to want something so bad that you make sacrifices. You keep going when you feel like quitting, but it is your desire for what you want that drives you through to success.

There once was a young man who was looking for the secret to success, and he met a highly successful person and asked him to teach him how to be successful. The successful man (teacher) stated, "Meet me at the beach at five in the morning and I will teach you."

As requested, the young man (student) appeared at the beach at the designated time the following morning.

The teacher stated, "Step out into the water ankle-deep."

The student did as he was told.

The teacher said, "Good, now let's go waist-high in the water."

The young man begrudgingly did but began to feel he was wasting his time, that the exercises he was performing were of little value in teaching him how to be successful.

The teacher said, "Now go in up to your chin."

1

The student was seriously beginning to get upset and felt this was a total waste of his time, energy, and effort; the teacher was not truly sharing the secrets of success with him. So the student began to voice his thoughts and asked the teacher to show him how to be successful or stop wasting his time.

The teacher grabbed the student's head and shoved it under the water, holding him there, and the student began to fight and struggle for air. The teacher let him up to breathe.

Furious at the teacher, the student demanded, "Why did you do that?"

The teacher stated, "When your desire to succeed is as strong as your will to breathe, you will be successful."

Succeed

As Bad As You Want To

Breathe

Then Then You Will be

Successful

Desire is a strong emotion. When we have a strong desire for something, we will not be denied. When we have desire, the universal intelligence that guides all things, pulls the desired thing, person, state of being, or element to be drawn inexorably like a magnet toward us. Our job is to prepare to receive the object of our desire into our lives. In the midst of pain, sacrifice, and commitment to our cause, we tend to fight through whatever adversity we are dealing with to satisfy our desire.

Olympic athletes are an excellent example of this. The training can be grueling, with ten- to fifteen-hour days over years, and they must work through pain and sometimes rehabilitation after painful injuries in order to accomplish their success. They forego fun and time with friends and family to accomplish their dreams. A driving desire is the core ingredient that pushes them through the pain and through the sacrifices that they so often need.

Sacrifices

Let's take a moment to understand the word *sacrifice*. Unwillingness and lack of courage and/or willpower to make the necessary sacrifices are often the killers of dreams. Many times the things we need to give up or let go of we choose not to. A dear friend once shared a quote that I often refer to: "We don't always want what we need." We often need to let go of the very things we don't want to lct go of or give up on. We have to make these hard choices if we want that desired life.

If there is a person, place, or thing that inhibits you from reaching your true potential and is unwilling to assist or even encourage you in achieving your goals, this is one of those moments you may have to make a tough choice and sacrifice to remove or change the inhibiting factor involved in the situation. Sometimes it's bad or irresponsible spending habits; sometimes it's a drug or alcohol addiction; sometimes it's bad eating habits; and sometimes we have to move to a different place, giving up what is familiar and known to us. But this is where you really need to understand what's important to you as an individual. What are your ethical standards? What things do you value and place priority on? This is one of those areas where a wrong decision could be detrimental to you and your well-being. But only you can decide, and a decisive decision is necessary to move you forward to your dream life.

I once read a quote by Bill Gates, describing one of his guiding principles for making Microsoft so successful. He stated that he took massive decisive action on the decision he had to make. Some decisions you make will be right and some may be wrong, but the power lies in your deciding and then taking massive decisive action on it ... So evaluate yourselves and ask these most important questions:

- What are my desires?
- What are my passions?
- What are my values?
- What are my priorities?
- What are my ethical standards as they relate to my desired life?
- What sacrifices am I willing to make to reach my goal?

It is important to understand the answers to these questions. These answers will become the guiding barometer for those tough times. These questions will help you understand those things that may compromise your moral, business, and spiritual ethics as well as provide guidance to you in making the right decisions. You've surely heard the saying that a person who stands for nothing will fall for anything. So know your constitution, know what you will stand, fight, and sacrifice for.

I've found that many people don't know what their desires are. People always seem to tell us what they don't want, but if you listen closely, they never mention what they do want. People live their lives each day not recognizing the power they have over the moment, the power to make a difference in their lives and the lives of others whom they touch. Instead, they transfer their power to others to make the decisions for them. It is critical that you realize the power that you have in shaping your destiny.

God has given each of us a unique talent that is as specific to us as cells are to one's DNA. This talent, your gift, is to be shared with the world. It's your responsibility to develop your unique God-given gift. For some, it is easy to identify and develop that gift; others have to work at identifying and developing their gifts or talents.

Regardless of how easy or difficult it is to identify your gift, you must realize that you are unique to this earth and within you are precious jewels that only you are blessed to bestow upon others. For example, a diamond found in its natural state looks nothing like the diamonds we see in the jewelry stores. A diamond in its raw state looks like an ugly rock. Before it becomes that beautiful jewel, a diamond must go through a process. It should endure enormous pressure, fire, and heat. It must be developed. This is the same with your talent, your jewel.

To reach the full potential of your gifts, you must decide to develop those skills. It is a conscious decision to evolve and live our dream lives. A natural law applies here: "Every action has a reaction, even if there is no action at all." So your actions or lack of actions define those conscious decisions you make from moment to moment, which will determine your end results. Those quantitative results are the directives that will lead you to that desired life ... or not.

How do I find my desire? This question puzzles many individuals. There are strategies that you can use to define that desire. One strategy you could use is to first start with a self-evaluation. For thirty days, keep a log of the things you enjoy doing as well as those things that seem to be a chore or task for you, things you truly don't like doing. While keeping this log, ask people who know you well what they think your strongest characteristics and weakest characteristics are. Ask this question of your family members, your friends, and your coworkers. Keep a log of their responses and evaluate that against what you enjoy doing and what you don't enjoy doing. This is an excellent way to flush out your true desire. You will find that those things that are sometime the easiest to do or the things you enjoy the most could be your desire. There are no guarantees, but this is where it starts for those who are serious about living their desired lives.

Once you have identified your true desire, it is time to develop those skills. Move boldly on these characteristics and develop these skill sets. Look for specialized training in those areas that you have identified. Read everything you can find on the subject matter. Interview and talk to people who are already in that field. Your *commitment* to learning and developing the skills sets required is so focus it becomes your goal to evolve into a recognized leader in your chosen field of study. This process won't happen overnight. It requires a commitment of time, energy, and resources. But keep things in perspective. We are talking about engineering the life you deserve, a life that will be fulfilled with a lifetime of happiness and balance. So begin acting today!

The starting point of all achievement is desire. Keep this constantly in mind.

Weak desire, brings weak results.

As a small amount of fire makes a small amount of heat.

—Napoleon Hill

Notes

Chapter 2

Principle of Passion

What exactly is passion? How do you know when you have passion for something? These are just a couple of questions that people may ask themselves. The dictionary describes passion as "a strong feeling of enthusiasm or excitement for doing something or about doing something." To live the desired life, passion is essential. Your true passion reflects the love you have for the innate gift that you have been born with, those works that bring you the greatest senses of accomplishment and joy. You do them not because of the money you can earn but because they feel so natural. Those things don't feel like work.

My stepfather, Talmadge Gibson, was such a man. He was a pianist and loved to play big band jazz music. Some days he would play for hours upon hours, never playing the same song twice. Watching him play, one could see and feel the passion he had for playing the piano. He would sometimes serenade my mother, who is visually impaired, and she would dance around the house and sing with him. They were living the desired life.

My grandparents owned a flower shop for over sixty years. They had the passion of designing and arranging flowers in an artistic way. Sometimes they would work all night long, and as a young man, I would wonder how they did it. It wasn't like work for them. They loved the work that they did, and they brought happiness to thousands of people over the years, whether they were arranging flowers for the loss of a loved one, the marriage of a couple, or the birth of a newborn baby. They made a difference. It was their passion, and everyone around them could tell.

There are many such stories in your community. It is always clear which people are walking with their passion. They do what they do for the love of it. Each of us has within us that special thing that brings happiness and joy to the world.

Your passion is the vehicle that allows you to have the potential power to influence and make a difference in the world of all those who encounter your unique gifts and work. Your passion has a rippling effect on all those with whom you share it. This is the reason you should be passionate about what you do.

Just imagine if Benjamin Franklin had not been so curious and passionate about electrical storms. Our world today as we know it could have been very different. Do you think he thought that one day humans would be able to walk into a dark room and hit a light switch and the room would light up? I sincerely doubt it.

Imagine when the Wright brothers took that very first flight for about three hundred yards. Do you think they even thought about sheets of curved metal in an oval shape that would fly hundreds of people at a time to the other side of the world within hours? More than likely, they didn't even conceive of such a thing.

These are just a few examples of how your passion can changed and impact the lives of humanity. However, your passion doesn't have to affect people lives in such a monumental way. Your passion has impact on the small child who sees you passionately working every day or the neighborhood coach who enjoys transferring his learned skill to a group of youngsters. Whatever your passion is, it's important to share it. The rippling effect of your passion affects the outcome of others. Had Benjamin Franklin or the Wright brothers not had the courage to pursue their visions, we might still be in the dark ages. So let your passion be all it can be.

Passion is not about perfection, waiting for that perfect moment to occur. It's about transforming through your daily efforts (like the butterfly).

That's where perfect change occurs because of those small imperfect efforts made daily.

Notes

Chapter 3

Principle of Faith

Faith is fundamental to success. When we think about living our potential desired lives, we must have faith that God the Creator has supplied us with everything we need to be successful. Hebrews 11:1 shares the following verse: "Now faith is the substance of things hoped for, the evidence of things not seen."

We must have faith that we are one with the universe and are an intricate part of this creation called life. It is through this paradigm that we know our contributions to life are significant and have a rippling effect on all those that encounter our works. It's like dropping a pebble in a lake and watching the rippling tide grow from the center outward. The rippling effect changes the direction of each droplet of water forever, and so it is with you, potentially changing those lives you have encountered and made an impact on. Your family members, friends, and those who observe you from afar become inspired by your success. It is through this inspiration that we grow as individuals as well. However, it is our faith that gives us the courage to act boldly on our thoughts. In the Bible, Matthew verse 17:20 states the following: "If ye have faith as a grain of mustard seed, ye shall say unto this mountain, remove hence to yonder place; and it shall remove and nothing shall be impossible unto you." You see, someone has moved mountains, tunnels have been carved through them, and roads have been built over them. The people who first thought of these things only had a dream, a vision, and the willpower to see those dreams and vision through to the end. So I challenge you to have the faith and confidence that your Creator has given you everything needed to engineer the life you deserve.

You may have heard this expression: "What we think and concentrate most on is what materializes in our lives." This is such a true statement. Our thoughts reflect our faith or lack of faith that God, our Creator, has provided everything we need to accomplish our dream lives. This is played out in our daily lives through our routines.

Faith is to believe what you do not see; the reward of this faith is to see what you believe.

-Saint Augustine

How many times have we desired something so much and had little chance of receiving it? But something extraordinary happens. We find ourselves so engaged in the thought of what we desire and suddenly the very thing we desire comes forth. The reason for this is that our thoughts and faith are so strong that those things we desire are drawn to us. The reason is that we begin to act in faith. Our physical actions begin to display that faith, and the universal law of attraction begins to respond to our behavior and actions. I read an unknown quote that stated, "We don't go to our dreams; our dreams come to us." Some call it destiny. But I believe those things we think most about are what we attract in our world. Our actions are a mirrored reflection of our mental thoughts.

15

Faith gives you the courage to act. In the movie *Raiders of the Lost Ark*, there was a scene where Indiana Jones had to cross a bottomless ravine. There was not a visible bridge to the other side of the ravine. However, in the secret map that he possessed, there was an invisible bridge that would appear only after he had taken the first step off the cliff. I'm not suggesting you step off a cliff, but metaphorically speaking, going after your dream life has similarities. It has the feel of taking the leap of faith. You don't always know if you are going to make it to the other side, but there is one thing for sure: if you don't try, you will never make it to the other side. Therefore, act with courage and faith; know that in your heart, your mind, and your spirit that your Creator (God) has given you everything you need to achieve your desired life.

Nothing is impossible;

the word itself says

"I'm possible!"

—Audrey Hepburn

Notes

Chapter 4

Principle of Belief

What is belief? Belief is an acceptance that a statement is true or that something exists. It's a trust, faith, or confidence in someone or something. We all have heard the phrase that if you don't believe in what you are doing, no one else will either. Or consider this one: "If you can believe it, you can achieve it." These metaphoric statements have power. They have the power to transcend one's thoughts and ideas into tangible actions. Without our belief mechanism, we would not have the courage or strength to tackle the ideas and thoughts that we have been blessed with. It is through our belief in our abilities and our faith in a higher power that our visionary thoughts are released and the ability to dream the impossible dream is realized.

Many people ask, "What's the difference between faith and belief?" There is a fundamental difference between faith and belief. Faith is the belief in things you don't yet see, but you act upon them with the faith that your Creator has provided you with everything you need to succeed. Belief is seeing and believing that you have the ability to bring about any tools, resources, and needs required to bring forth your desired results. It's about believing in your own ability and skill set to either accomplish the goal yourself or accept the responsibility of galvanizing the talents needed to accomplish the goal.

Either way, your belief in your ability to bring forth the actions necessary to accomplish your dream is a direct result of your ability to believe in yourself.

In James Allen's book *Above Life's Turmoil*, he states that we won't attempt something unless we have the belief that we can accomplish it. He says that belief always precedes action. This is a very powerful concept to understand. Knowing you have the power to alter your thoughts and change your belief allows you to act and alter your destiny.

By altering our attitudes, we can alter our lives.

—Zig Ziglar

Dr. Wayne Dyer, writing in *You'll See It When You Believe It*, says your behavior is based upon feelings that are based upon your thoughts. He states that the thing to work on is not your behavior but those things inside your consciousness that we call thoughts. If you change your thoughts, you change your actions. Our thoughts reflect those things we genuinely want to accomplish. Once we believe in those thoughts, our actions automatically become aligned with our thoughts. Our thoughts control our actions, and until we believe in those thoughts, we won't have that burning desire to act.

Only your thoughts and actions can determine your life.

—TheLawOfAttraction.com

We all have had moments where we could see our desires but for some reason would not go for them because we didn't believe we would be successful. We didn't believe we had the ability or resources required to accomplish the objective. An old adage by Henry Ford says, "Whether you think you can or whether you think you can't, you're right." So you choose the cup. Is the cup half-empty, or is it half-full? Both perceptions are correct. Ultimately, the path you choose is a direct reflection of your belief in your ability to bring about a successful conclusion.

Henry Ford instructed his engineers to design the horseless carriage, and they all stated it was impossible. Henry Ford refused to believe it was impossible. He inspired his team of engineers to believe in his vision, and thus the horseless carriage was born, which we know as the automobile.

The power of belief makes the seemingly impossible, possible. Think about the times in your own life when nobody believed you could accomplish a certain act. Think about the times you were doubted and you went on to prove that you were right because your convictions and beliefs were so powerful that you refused to fail. Think about how strong your thoughts were.

Our thoughts and beliefs have power. Everything exists because people had thoughts or ideas and the belief in their abilities to bring forth their thoughts and/or ideas. The point that I am making is that you have that same power. Believe in your God-given talents. Make an honest effort to develop your skills to the best of your ability and pull the trigger. Your dream life is within your grasp. You are the commander of your ship.

When you develop yourself to the point where your belief in yourself is so strong that you know you can accomplish anything you put your mind to, your future will be unlimited.

—Brian Tracy

Chapter 5

Principle of Action

Action is the fuel and energy that perpetuates and brings forth the dream into a physical presence. One can have the above four principles (desire, passion, faith, and belief), but the dream can never materialize without action. A biblical proverb says, "Faith without work is dead." It's through this energy (the principle of action) that our efforts begin to breathe life and take form.

When we say the principles of action, what exactly does this mean? It means that you have thought about your objectives, your goals, and your purpose. You have planned a key set of specific tasks that must be accomplished to bring about the dream life you desire. It means acting upon those specific tasks in a deliberate and intentional manner that will move you from point A to point B.

Take action! An inch of movement will bring you closer to your goals than a mile of intention.

—Dr. Steve Maraboli

Many people act, but many times it's not deliberate or intentional. For example, you could wake up tomorrow in California and say, "You know, I feel like driving to New York today." You get dressed, hop in the car, and begin driving in the direction you think New York would be. This is not deliberate or intentional; it is being spontaneous. You may or may not get to New York. But it won't be in the most efficient manner, and the odds are against a successful outcome. The road trip will be filled with many unnecessary obstacles to overcome because you did not have a plan of action or road map to direct you for the best route to take. This is exactly what happens in life.

A quote states, "We can plan to fail by failing to plan." This is so true, and the choice is always there for us to choose. Therefore, we should choose our actions wisely.

One of the first and most important action steps that we should take is to create a mental vision of that desired life. The clearer the vision, the greater the chance of success. The following outlines a few of these important steps.

First create a visual picture of what your desired life will look like. Physically write the vision out. Put it on paper and be as detailed as you can. Read and visualize the vision, and imprint the vision in your mind daily. Do it first thing in the morning, and then visualize it many times throughout the day, also making it the last thing you do at night. Keep the following in mind:

- Remember that you can adjust it as necessary.
- Commit to the successful completion of the plan.
- Know that quitting is not an option.

These are powerful steps. They can transform your thoughts into a dominating belief that will drive your actions. There is a saying that whatever our most dominate thoughts are is what we attract into our lives. Therefore, by taking these steps, you are empowering your mind to create the energy, effort, and commitment to overcome any obstacles that may interfere with the obtainment of your goals and objectives.

I remember one hot, sunny afternoon in North Carolina when I was cutting the grass with my four-year-old grandson. All that week I had been teaching him and repeating to him a conceptual quote: "Winners never quit, and quitters never win." On this day, it was so hot and I could not continue cutting the grass. But my grandson was enjoying pushing the lawn mower with me. He did not want to stop. He then said to me, "Granddaddy, winners never quit, and quitters never win." This four-year-old grandchild of mine got it. He did not want to stop cutting that grass, and he reminded me of the quote I had been drilling into him all week. I had to keep going; I had to finish. The moral of the story is to find what is important to you. Find your *why*. My grandson was my reason, and what I was trying to teach him was a driving force for me to finish cutting that grass.

Do not underestimate yourself. Remember, without your presence, someone else's life won't be complete.

—kushandwizdom.tumblr

We often procrastinate on the action required to bring about a successful outcome. Why do we hesitate on creating our desired lives? Is it because we don't have the belief or confidence in our ability to accomplish the task? Is it because we are afraid we will fail? Is it because we feel we lack the required resources to bring about a successful ending? These are just a few of the many reasons we procrastinate. However, we can overcome procrastination. We must take one step at a time. We should take baby steps. Another metaphoric quote applies here: "How do you eat an elephant one bite at a time?" The metaphor simply means that in developing or creating your desired life, just take one action at a time. Concentrate only on that next step that you need to take. If you apply this simple technique, you will one day look back and say to yourself, "Wow, look at what I have accomplished."

Fear is one of the major reasons we don't act on our dreams. It comes in many different forms. Fear paralyzes your forward momentum. It's like a surfer sitting in the calmest ocean aboard a surfboard, waiting for the perfect wave to come. But the wave never comes and the surfer just drifts along with the current of the water. In life, many of us are waiting for that perfect time or moment to act, but the moment never comes and we drift along with the currents of life. Then we look back one day and realize just how much time we have wasted. But even in spite of this awareness, you should also realize that today is the first day of the rest of your life and it's never too late to start creating your desired life today.

I've learned that we do have power over what we do in life. We may not have power over circumstances or the cards that we've been dealt, but we certainly have power over how we play the hand we've been dealt. It has to do with a person's perspective and how one sees things. You can look at life and be pessimistic or you can decide to be optimistic. For example, you have a glass of water that is equally half-empty or equally half-full. You can choose to view the glass of water in one of two ways: one as half-empty, which could potentially create a mind-set that is rooted in the spirit of lack; or two, view the half glass of water as half-full, which has the mind-set that is rooted in the spirit of abundance.

Both mind-sets are correct. There is no right or wrong in this situation. It's just a perspective that will determine the actions you will or will not take. It all relates back to your

25

belief system. However, what's important to understand in this example is the subset of actions you will take based on the core root of your mind-set and perspective. One mind-set is firmly rooted in a mind-set of abundance, and the other is firmly rooted in the mind-set of lack.

The subconscious mind-set will create either an attitude of confidence or an attitude that lacks the confidence you need to take decisive action. I once read an article on Bill Gates speaking of when he first founded Microsoft. Mr. Gates stated that the only difference between Microsoft and his competitors was that he took decisive action on his goals and objectives. The decision to act in the manner that he did has now made him one of the wealthiest men in the world. I point this out because his mind-set had to be that of abundance. He saw the half-empty glass as half-full instead of half-empty. It is imperative that you understand the source of your actions. Are your actions driven by spirit of an abundant mind-set or are they driven by a mind-set that is filled with the spirit of lack?

This is important to understand. You are what you think you are. Your dominate thoughts are like the seeds of a fruit plant. If you plant an orange tree seed and nurture and care for the orange tree seed, it will produce oranges one day in the future. It cannot produce apples because the seed was not an apple tree but an orange tree. Therefore, if your dominant thoughts and beliefs are of an abundant mind-set, your immediate actions will be in alignment with doing what's necessary to bring forth abundant actions. Your dominant thoughts drive your immediate actions. Simply stated, if you feel you can't do something, you are probably right. If you feel you can do something, you are probably right again. Act today and begin to build that desired life. You can do it!

Notes

Chapter 6

Principle of Reevaluation

When creating their desired lives, many people will give into the normal pressures of life and give up on their dreams. They have planned it out, put in some effort and action, but it didn't work out as planned. They may have even modified the plan a bit but it still didn't work out. This is when that feeling of doubt begins to raise its ugly head. We begin to lack the confidence and courage to move past this point. But this is exactly the opposite of what one should do.

Chances of success:

I won't:	0 percent
I can't:	10 percent
I don't know how:	20 percent
I wish I could:	30 percent
I want to:	40 percent
I think I might:	50 percent
I might:	60 percent
I think I can:	70 percent
I can:	80 percent

I am doing it:　　　　90 percent

I did it:　　　　　　100 percent

Creating your desired life is not a straight line. There are many twists and turns in engineering your desired life. We should embrace and evaluate the changes required. Consider the quote that there are many ways to skin a cat. Just know that some ways are better than others are.

The road to success is not straight.
- There is a curve called failure.
- A loop called confusion.
- Speed bumps called friends.
- Red lights called enemies.
- Caution lights called family.
- You will have flat tires called jobs.

But,
- If you have a spare called determination,
- An engine called perseverance,
- A driver called willpower,

You will make it to a place called success.

—unknown

Many people reject change and stretching themselves outside of their comfort zone. But creating a desired life, you are constantly outside of your comfort zone. You are constantly evaluating your yearly, monthly, and even daily results. The winds of change require this of you. Whenever a plane is in flight, part of the job of being a pilot is to evaluate the status of the aircraft. The pilot is constantly evaluating whether the plane is operating properly and is flying in the direction it should be. If for some reason the aircraft is not performing the way it is supposed to, the pilot will make the necessary adjustments. The pilot may even have to go back to where the plane took off to have the adjustments made. However, the clear majority of the time, the destination is completed.

If we look back in history, we will see hundreds, if not thousands, of examples of individuals challenging themselves to create a better life for themselves, their families, and their communities. I think of people like Dr. Martin Luther King, who led a nation of people and a country to embrace civil rights and justice for all its citizens. Think about the insurmountable odds and circumstances he had to overcome. Imagine the constant evaluation and sacrifice that he had to make. This was no easy task by any measure. Because of his efforts and willingness to stand up in the face of life-threatening circumstances, the Civil Rights Act was created and passed and millions of individuals who had no right to vote on the government that would be governing their lives would now have that right. Nearly fifty years later, America had the opportunity to embrace its first African American president. What a dream this was for so many people to see.

As in the previous example, your real power lies in your ability to hold true to your core values and evaluate as circumstances require. Dr. Martin Luther King's core values were equal rights, and he did not succumb to the current powers of the day. He accepted finite disappointments, but he never loss infinite hope.

We must accept finite disappointment, but never lose infinite hope.

—Martin Luther King Jr.

You have that same power within you to create your desired life. It's not an easy task, but it is a possible task. Greatness is not reserves for any one individual. It's reserved for those who are willing to do what is necessary with integrity to overcome their individual challenges.

I think about Muhammad Ali, the greatest boxer of all time. But his true greatness was not because of his boxing. It was because of his willingness to stand up against a government that wanted to draft him into an unjustified war and he refused to go. Thus they stripped him of his championship belt and imprisoned him during his prime boxing years. His imprisonment brought attention to a war that was unjustified and eventually a draft system that would soon be dismantled. Upon Muhammad Ali's release from prison, he regained his championship belt three times. He had to evaluate his style of boxing because Father Time was beginning to catch up with him. He was known for "Float like a butterfly, sting like a bee." He then adjusted to a style he created, which was called rope-a-dope.

These are just a couple of examples of how you see the principle of evaluation being instrumental in creating power in the lives of these men—their ability to evaluate and adjust to circumstances that would have crushed the dreams and hopes of those men and women who couldn't hold true to their core values and adjust with integrity.

Therefore, as you begin to take on the task of creating your desired life and you encounter those challenges that you will most certainly meet, begin to think about how you need to evaluate and adjust. As you are evaluating, ask yourself these questions:

1. What are my core values?
2. Are the adjustments in line with my core values?
3. Can I make these changes with integrity?

31

These guiding questions are not all the questions you should ponder but a beginning dialogue with yourself to help you engineer the life you deserve.

Don't Dream your life, Live Your Dreams.

Notes

Chapter 7

Principle of Adjustment

We often verbalize words without understanding the true meaning and the impact those words may have on us, our community, and/or our society. With that said, let's analyze the word *adjustment*. The Google dictionary defines the word as follows: a small alteration or movement made to achieve a desired fit, appearance, or result; the process of adapting or becoming used to a new situation.

There is power in understanding just how impactful this one principle can be in engineering your desired life. This principle is the glue that brings all of the other concepts together (desire, passion, faith, belief, action, and evaluation). This principle allows your desired life to develop in spite of the potential obstacles that could derail your dreams. The principle of adjustment is the action that displays your passion, faith, and your belief in your dream by living on through those moments when you feel like giving up on the desired goal. The action of making a small alteration or movement here or there is what keeps the dream alive. We should plan for and expect to adjust to new situations that threaten the very existence of our desired lives.

The pessimist complains
about the wind.

The optimist expects
it to change.

The realist adjusts the sail.

—William A. Ward

Imagine the impact of a small alteration or movement allowing you to make a difference in the lives of those who would not have experienced the gift that only you could have given them. Envision how your developed gift or talent affects the lives of those who support and believe in your vision. Adjustment is the tool that allows your vision to flourish and your goals to thrive. Without the principle of adjustment, we could possibly give in to a self-defeating attitude—an attitude of frustration, disappointment, and the feeling of failure. But the power of adjustment allows us to overcome this feeling of despair. Everything begins with the proper mind-set. Most successful people envision how things will be first. They start with the end in mind. We've all heard the saying that a picture is worth a thousand words. This is so true.

Nothing has the power to radically change a life more than an attitude adjustment.

—Gail Lynn Goodwin

When you encountered the eight-hundred-pound gorilla that is attempting to kill your dream, you simply don't give up on the dream; you make the necessary adjustments. It's important that we understand how valuable this concept is. Your dream is like a seed, a jewel, a buried treasure that the Creator chose to implant in your realm of reality. This treasured gift is your responsibility to develop for you, your family, your community, and society. When you fail to cultivate and share these treasures you possess, you potentially rob the world of the legacy of your contributions.

The principle of adjustment allows your commitment to your dream to excel and achieve the life you've always desired. However, it all begins with the proper mind-set of

"Yes, we can." It doesn't matter where you are now. What matters is where you believe you can go and what you believe you can do.

Any number of circumstances can require you to adjust. The timing could be wrong, the industry could have changed, or the political environment could not be suitable for your product or service. Whatever the reason, the key is to have the proper mind-set and an open mind and be willing to evolve with the circumstances. With that in mind, you must know what your core beliefs are and understand how they may change as well.

It reminds me of when typewriters were the primary business tool before the computer revolution and the Information Age. I was watching a person on an airplane working on her iPad, typing with just two index fingers. I then pondered how things had changed and how she had adjusted from the era of the typewriter. You would never use just those two fingers to type. This is just a small example of how things change; we must adjust to whatever the current situation is.

Many people refuse to adjust. They have always done things a certain way, and this is the only way they will ever do those things. This attitude is a closed-minded attitude and an attitude of limited growth. If you choose not to adjust, you are choosing the way of the dinosaur. Then the natural law of entropy will take hold. If you don't expand, you will cease to exist, just like the dinosaur.

The principle of adjustment requires growth. It requires the desire, the will, and the ability to expand beyond the current knowledge base you may possess. I once read a quote by Sydney J. Harris:

A winner knows how much he still has to learn, even when he is considered an expert by others.

A loser wants to be considered an expert by others before he has learned enough to know how little he knows.

Winners	Losers
Say, "It may be difficult, but it is possible."	Say, "It may be possible, but it is too difficult."
See the gain.	See the pain.
See possibilities.	See problems.
Make it happen.	Let it happen.

The understanding of this quote and concept is extremely powerful. It allows you to embrace the fact that you should continue to grow and learn. It embraces the fact that you should continually challenge the limits of your existing knowledge and look to broaden and expand your horizon.

Knowledge comes in all forms and formats. It doesn't always have to be in a formal educational format. Knowledge is constantly around, and we should have an attitude of openness to absorb, learn, and execute the knowledge we acquire. There is a quote that knowledge is power, and this is true to some degree. But it is missing one very important adjective. The one word that is missing is *applied*. "Applied knowledge is power." As we acquire, investigate, and apply our newfound knowledge into implementation, it automatically activates the principle of adjustment. It allows us to see and view things from a different perspective. It empowers us to negotiate the wave of change with a confidence we may have lacked. The principle of adjustment embodies the vision of our dreams and allows us to manifest those dreams through our actions. If we act boldly, move confidently, and think definitively, we will engineer the life we deserve.

Notes

Chapter 8

Conclusion

The purpose of this book is to inspire you to visualize your possibilities, develop your potential, and realize the fullness of your capabilities. These traits are innate to all who choose to engage their God-given power and talents. But your doctrine requires you to heighten your ability by increasing your knowledge and realize that you are a unique individual. Be aware that you a have special purpose on this planet, regardless of your circumstances. Your presence does make a difference. Your ability to act within the realm of your interests releases within you the power to create the world you desire while making a difference in the lives of others.

You will get all you want in life if you help enough other people get what they want.

—Zig Ziglar

Live your life to its fullest, and contribute to make your home, community, and society a better place. Let that creation begin within you. Someone once said, "Be the change you want to see." You don't have to be great to start, but you must start for you to be great.

Be the change you wish to see in the world!

Living the life you deserve is not easy to obtain, and it is reserved for those who have the courage and confidence to live life on their own terms and act. This is where the connection between your faith and belief unite and work in unison as one entity. Have faith that the Creator (God) has supplied you with everything you need to succeed, and believe in your God-given ability to overcome any obstacle you may face.

Courage is defined as the quality of mind or spirit that enables a person to face difficulty.

Confidence is defined as the belief in one's self and one's power or abilities to overcome obstacles.

This means that your ability to think, move, and act boldly is demonstrated by how strong your courage is in your faith and how tenacious your confidence is in your belief in your ability to bring about the desired results.

Each day think of your desires and passions, and include in those thoughts how you make a difference in the world for those you encounter. Think about how life may have been different in their worlds if you had not the courage to be all you can be. Each of us has the power to be a game changer. Greatness is not reserved for any one individual. We all can hit the game-winning shot. But that talent is a developed talent, a developed skilled, and it is your choice to decide whether you would like to develop that skill or talent.

Greatness is not what you become,

It's what you Overcome.

When we see individuals living the dream life, we often think that they are incredibly lucky. We see their lives from the outside looking in and may not truly understand the sacrifices, commitment, and challenges that they had to overcome. With each level of success come levels of sacrifices, challenges, and commitments. However, the prize of overcoming these commitments, challenges, and sacrifices is so worth the reward for the family, community, and society in general. We all become winners when our goals are bigger than our own personal objectives.

Therefore, have the courage, confidence, and strength of character to chase your desires and live your passion. Have enough faith that your Creator gave you everything necessary to win. Believe in your innate ability to find and utilize the resources that abundantly surround you like hidden diamonds waiting for you to discover them. Take action on those dreams, and as you progress, evaluate your success and make the necessary adjustments. As you apply the seven principles to engineer the life you deserve, you will look back one day in awe of how you are the creator.

Dare to live the life you have dreamed for yourself. Go forward and make your dreams come true.

—Ralph Waldo Emerson

Begin the process of visualizing, defining, and applying the principles to engineer the life you deserve. The following pages provide a journal for you to meditate and log your daily expectations for the next thirty days. There are no wrong or right answers just your personal desires, goals, and dreams. The more detailed you describe your thoughts and visions the greater the opportunity of accomplishing the desired results.

Start this process first thing each morning in a place of solitude with a prayer and meditation of gratitude. Express to your Creator just how thankful you are for your gifts you possess, and the opportunity to make a difference in the lives of others. While meditating visualize and think about the following points:

- What your expectations of the day should be.
- Envision how you expect your day to go.
- Who you expect your day to impact.
- Why your actions are important.

Regardless of what level of prominence or prestige you've obtain in your life, you do make a difference and bring value to your sphere of influence. This prayer and meditation period allows you to bond with a higher level of consciousness and connect with the universal law of expectation. This is where your God given talents you've been blessed with are unleashed. You will begin each day with a clearly defined purpose and vision.

The steps of prayer and meditation are critically important steps and should not be taken lightly. This process allows your actions to be in alignment with your thoughts daily. Many times the actions we take have little or no benefit to accomplishing our goals. By having a clear vision and plan of action you will eliminate the wasted energy and resources. So take time each morning and begin your day with a prayer and meditation.

We are communicating about a *lifetime* of high achievement. Accomplishing this level of achievement requires a dedicated level of commitment to yourself. A commitment so strong that you will do what is necessary to accomplish your goal. It's a fight that you are committed to winning, because failure is not an option. Be reminded that failure most times only occurs when you decide to quit and give up. Your thirty day journal to *creating the life you deserve* begins now.

Day 1

- Desire

- Passion

- Faith

- Beliefs

- Actions

- Reevaluate

- Adjustment

Day 2

- Desire

- Passion

- Faith

- Beliefs

- Actions

- Reevaluate

- Adjustment

Day 3

- Desire

- Passion

- Faith

- Beliefs

- Actions

- Reevaluate

- Adjustment

Day 4

- Desire

- Passion

- Faith

- Beliefs

- Actions

- Reevaluate

- Adjustment

Day 5

- Desire

- Passion

- Faith

- Beliefs

- Actions

- Reevaluate

- Adjustment

Day 6

- Desire

- Passion

- Faith

- Beliefs

- Actions

- Reevaluate

- Adjustment

Day 7

- Desire

- Passion

- Faith

- Beliefs

- Actions

- Reevaluate

- Adjustment

Day 8

- Desire

- Passion

- Faith

- Beliefs

- Actions

- Reevaluate

- Adjustment

Day 9

- Desire

- Passion

- Faith

- Beliefs

- Actions

- Reevaluate

- Adjustment

Day 10

- Desire

- Passion

- Faith

- Beliefs

- Actions

- Reevaluate

- Adjustment

Day 11

- Desire

- Passion

- Faith

- Beliefs

- Actions

- Reevaluate

- Adjustment

Day 12

- Desire

- Passion

- Faith

- Beliefs

- Actions

- Reevaluate

- Adjustment

Day 13

- Desire

- Passion

- Faith

- Beliefs

- Actions

- Reevaluate

- Adjustment

Day 14

- Desire

- Passion

- Faith

- Beliefs

- Actions

- Reevaluate

- Adjustment

Day 15

- Desire

- Passion

- Faith

- Beliefs

- Actions

- Reevaluate

- Adjustment

Day 16

- Desire

- Passion

- Faith

- Beliefs

- Actions

- Reevaluate

- Adjustment

Day 17

- Desire

- Passion

- Faith

- Beliefs

- Actions

- Reevaluate

- Adjustment

Day 18

- Desire

- Passion

- Faith

- Beliefs

- Actions

- Reevaluate

- Adjustment

Day 19

- Desire

- Passion

- Faith

- Beliefs

- Actions

- Reevaluate

- Adjustment

Day 20

- Desire

- Passion

- Faith

- Beliefs

- Actions

- Reevaluate

- Adjustment

Day 21

- Desire

- Passion

- Faith

- Beliefs

- Actions

- Reevaluate

- Adjustment

Day 22

- Desire

- Passion

- Faith

- Beliefs

- Actions

- Reevaluate

- Adjustment

Day 23

- Desire

- Passion

- Faith

- Beliefs

- Actions

- Reevaluate

- Adjustment

Day 24

- Desire

- Passion

- Faith

- Beliefs

- Actions

- Reevaluate

- Adjustment

Day 25

- Desire

- Passion

- Faith

- Beliefs

- Actions

- Reevaluate

- Adjustment

Day 26

- Desire

- Passion

- Faith

- Beliefs

- Actions

- Reevaluate

- Adjustment

Day 27

- Desire

- Passion

- Faith

- Beliefs

- Actions

- Reevaluate

- Adjustment

Day 28

- Desire

- Passion

- Faith

- Beliefs

- Actions

- Reevaluate

- Adjustment

Day 29

- Desire

- Passion

- Faith

- Beliefs

- Actions

- Reevaluate

- Adjustment

Day 30

- Desire

- Passion

- Faith

- Beliefs

- Actions

- Reevaluate

- Adjustment

Printed in the United States
By Bookmasters